Cottingley

Cottingley

Alison Littlewood

NewCon Press
England

First published in the UK by NewCon Press
41 Wheatsheaf Road, Alconbury Weston, Cambs, PE28 4LF
July 2017

NCP 125 (limited edition hardback)
NCP 126 (softback)

10 9 8 7 6 5 4 3 2 1

ISBN:

978-1-910935-49-1 (hardback)
978-1-910935-50-7 (softback)

Cover art by Vincent Sammy
Cover layout by Andy Bigwood

Minor editorial meddling by Ian Whates
Book layout by Storm Constantine

3ʳᵈ September 1921

Dear Sir Arthur Conan Doyle,

Forgive the impertinence of my writing to you as a stranger and without introduction. I have lately exchanged correspondence with Mr Edward L. Gardner, and he would have been pleased to be our intermediary; but I felt that in view of your current endeavours, I should not delay in setting before you the wonders it has been my lot to discover.

I am aware that you have unveiled upon the world some photographs in which have been captured, by the agency and innocence of children, the little beings that live all about us and are usually unseen, which we have been pleased to name 'fairies'. Naturally, Mr Gardner, whom I had heard of a little through his lectures in Theosophy, hesitated to admit to me any particulars of your continued interest in the matter. I trust that, when I reveal the reason, you will feel his change of heart understandable, and I hope accept it as his only sensible course.

I hold within my hand something that will be of the utmost interest to you, if not the crowning exhibit in the proofs it may be your pleasure to unleash upon the disbelieving world. I will come to it, but first I will explain how it came to me, and say that I myself have undergone the most profound change of view regarding the existence of such beings, so that I hope I may be the model of what is to come upon a larger stage.

I am, I should say, too old for fairies. I am indeed the grandfather to a little girl, Harriet, who is seven years old. Sadly, the war visited me with the deepest grief with regards my son – my wife was spared such misfortune, having gone to a better place some years previously. My son's wife, Charlotte, and his child have done me the honour of abiding with me for the last few years, greatly to my comfort. I gave up my little business in the architectural line soon after the event and moved to a pleasant cottage just outside the village of Cottingley, with which I know you are familiar, for such is where the fairies were apparently captured on a photographic plate.

You may think that such circumstance would mean that Harriet had caught tales of the 'folk' from the local children, and it is true that she had heard tell of them, but little more. She is rather younger than Frances Griffiths and much more so than Elsie Wright, the two amateur photographers who brought the sprites to your notice, and being new to the village, she has often been somewhat rebuffed as an 'incomer' by those who should be her playfellows. Furthermore, we have discovered there to be a marked disinclination to speak on the subject of fairies among the residents hereabouts, one which has passed, rather more surprisingly, to their children.

And so it was with much enthusiasm, but nothing in the way of formed notions or expectation, that Harriet persuaded me to go 'hunting for fairies' in Cottingley Glen earlier this year.

Wishing to please her, and to allay in some wise the loneliness in her situation at which I have hinted, I set out readily enough. We had been there often before: she enjoys naming the flowers, and arranging pebbles in the stream, and peeking into birds' nests. It is a pretty place, and hearing her laughter and her chatter of magical things is pleasant for a fellow of my more sober years; and I smiled as I went, listening to the babble of Cottingley Beck and child alike.

There is a place – I understand Miss Wright has spoken of it also, though you have not yet found opportunity to visit – where the brook falls in merry little steps into the pools below. All about is verdure, with an abundance of wildflowers and singing birds, and the trees lower their branches, as if to provide a resting place for any travellers who wish to pause and admire and hang their legs over the stream. I did so, being rather more fatigued than Harriet, who busied herself poking twigs into the hollows to 'seek them out'.

She soon alarmed me, however, with a shriek, and I looked up sharply to see her whitened face, and a flash of light which I took for a reflection dancing in the water.

Tears started into her eyes. She held up a hand, staring at it, and at first I saw nothing; then a drop of crimson appeared at the knuckle and dripped into the pool. I hurried towards her, thinking she would begin to cry in earnest, but she appeared too surprised to do so. I caught her arm, drawing her up the banking, and examined the wound. Thankfully I found only a small, circular puncture, nothing concerning, and indeed she seemed to have forgotten all about it, for she pulled away and slithered down the banking again. She dirtied her dress as she went, and landed with her feet in the stream.

I was rather inclined to scold her, but she stood there with her back to me, so intent on something in her view she did not hear my words. I called her name; she remained motionless. This absence of attention was concerning. She was not accustomed to ignore her elders or to disregard their imprecations, but since she still did not turn I became curious and stepped towards her.

She was peering at a rock that jutted from the beck where it fell a matter of three or four feet to the pool in which she stood. The outcrop was darkened with spray and dressed with moss, though its upper surface remained relatively dry. There, tiny white flowers wavered in the humidity thrown up by the water. I could not see what had so interested my grandchild. I thought to find there some bee or wasp or other stinging thing, and then I blinked, for where the air was misted I thought I caught sight of a hazy form. It was like the tiny semblance of a man, but so indistinct I was certain I must be mistaken.

I forgot myself so much as to take another step, which soaked me to the ankle, but I did not look away until another bright flash caught my eye. This was to the side, and again could have been nothing but sunlight playing on water, except that when I looked at it directly I saw six or seven of the brightest, smallest, most lovely of beings, floating about us in the air.

Harriet's laughter added to the atmosphere of wonder and awe that came over me at the sight. My eyes are not what they once were, but when I peered more intently I made out the most perfect little ladies, their hair like gossamer and their wings iridescent like those of a butterfly. They captured the light and threw it back, now in lavender, now mauve, now in the palest of pinks.

Harriet called to them and stretched out her hands as if to provide a perch for them to land upon, but they did not; they drew away and, instead, she began to follow them. The strangeness – nay, the sheer peculiarity of it, the sense of falling into a dream, was such that I reached out and seized her shoulder. And something – oh, I do not know what, but something made me turn from such gorgeous little miracles and back to the grey stone.

There was something: I knew not what, but I leaned in closer. And I saw a little man all dressed in green, not six inches high. I did not see if he possessed wings like the others, for his expression caught my attention utterly. His pippin face was unreadable, but his eyes, which were quite black – and, if I may say it of such lovely perfection, somewhat soulless – were brilliant with anger, which deepened when he saw me looking at him.

The sight froze me to the place, and I became conscious of how cold it was, standing with my feet in the pool; but I peered more closely, because I saw that he was not alone. He stood over a little body lying at his feet. It was another of the females – quite beautiful, but entirely motionless.

I could not help myself: I reached out and he leaped into the air with rage, landing once more on the rock in front of the prone figure. Harriet was beside me again and she let out another shriek at his motion but at the sound he seemed to despair, and in the next instant another bright flash marked his darting away. A series of little clicks, such as might be made by a bat, drew my attention towards where the gaily dancing maidens had been; but as if by some mutual consent, they too had passed from sight.

I fully expected his companion to have similarly disappeared, but she had not. She lay as before, indifferent to everything; for I saw that her breast did not move with any breath; nor did any animating principle enliven her features. Her eyes were closed, and I could not doubt that she had gone to whatever heaven awaited such creatures.

That was the moment when I realised I could return home, not merely with a fanciful tale, but carrying the proof of what I had seen.

With especial care, I bore up the tiny form. I hardly felt its weight. I asked Harriet to draw my handkerchief from my pocket and I fashioned a sling in which to carry it, anxious to avoid crushing her wings. I kept expecting the fairy to vanish beneath my coarse hands, or dissolve into ether, but she did not.

I cannot adequately explain the effect it had upon me. My powers of description pale before your own; I will only say that my wondering was matched by a peculiar sense of fear at seeing something that was thus far out of my experience or expectation. I became concerned at how rapidly my heart was beating – I am no longer a young man – but I had an odd aversion to lingering any longer by the beck. Indeed, I wished to be away from it, and the glen, as quickly as was practicable; and so, stealing away the bounty I had found there, I walked home with Harriet by my side, the child piping questions to which I possessed no answers. And I hope it is not too fanciful to say that as I went the very sky looked different to me, knowing that such beings live beneath it.

Now, justly, I am sure you would request of me what became of the fairy. This is the point where the observer of such a marvel should say it has indeed vanished into the air, leaving no trace behind, conveniently leaving their story to the credulity of the listener; but such is not the case.

I placed the frail body into a little wooden box. I somehow did not like to have it in the house, though it preyed on my mind constantly; so I placed it in an outbuilding to which only I possess a key. I thought often of the beck, but something kept me from returning thence; perhaps some fear that the fairies might follow me back to the cottage to find her.

I regularly looked in on the box, though again, something stopped me from opening it. It was not until a number of weeks afterwards that I felt I should intrude upon her little casket and see what had become of the fairy. I know little of the process of human decomposition, and even if I had, I do not suppose it would be directly comparable; but I rather dreaded witnessing the putrefaction of such a lovely thing and, I must confess, the fear had grown upon me that she might really have vanished. If she had, I think there would have been nothing left to me but to puzzle over the loss of my senses.

She had not vanished. She had putrefied, however, and I suspect more rapidly than a human might, but it was not hideous. It was, rather, fascinating in the extreme. Indeed, I examined the body more closely with the aid of a magnifying glass, feeling as if I had fallen into one of your Sherlock Holmes stories and turned detective.

Barely anything was left of her flesh. What remained had greyed and turned powdery, and there was a smell upon bending closely over it, like stale herbs. And beneath the skin – oh, what a splendid little skeleton! It is a wondrous thing, delicate as a bird's, and easily as weightless. She possesses ribs like a human's, though more steeply angular, as if crushed by the strictest corset. The leg bones seem very like, though I only noticed upon looking so closely that the knees bend backwards. The arms are similar to a woman's in everything but size, as is the skull, if a trifle elongated, like some of the more primitive incarnations of humanity. The wings are incredibly fragile, akin to those of a preserved insect. The roots of them remain and they are veined; they are quite whole, the membranes nearly transparent. My hand shakes as I write, it is so very strange and wonderful.

And so I come to the purpose of my letter. I have not told of the fairy to anyone save Mr Gardner and now yourself. Indeed, I scarcely know what to do. Here is a discovery that could open the eyes of man to something the like of which is unheard of in our history, and yet I fear I am not possessed of the skills or wherewithal to accomplish it. And so I write to you, Sir Arthur, most humbly, in recognition not only of your penmanship, which is of course without compare (I have read many of your praiseworthy stories, and even now Charlotte sits at my side, barely keeping in check her ardent admiration and good wishes), but also with regard to your high reputation, your unimpeachable character, and your interest in the world I have so unwittingly stumbled upon.

The skeleton, I am certain, will pass any inspection. It may be photographed; it may be examined, so long as such examination does not press it to destruction, for it is as fragile as may be supposed.

In short, I can only assure you what a singular object this is. I would be greatly honoured to set it before you at any date you require, and at your convenience. I am only sorry I cannot send it to you, but as I am certain you will understand, I fear to move her – she would crumble to dust, I think, or may be mislaid upon the way, and that would be the most tragic and unbearable loss.

For this is something that should belong to the whole world. Of course, the mind of man is such that when faced with an idea so new, the inclination is to see what one will and disregard anything that does not line up accordingly. But this – it must surely break through any such failure to see. It cannot be denied!

Needless to say – and the times are such that I must address a point that should require no assurances – I seek no monetary gain. I would merely see the remains set before those who may use them best for the advancement of Truth and Knowledge, and such things should never be sullied or brought into question by financial inducement.

I have exhausted my tale. Pray, forgive the length of my letter; having remained silent on the subject for so long, I am quite carried away by it. I dare hope you will be as excited as I with the discovery, and I most eagerly anticipate your reply.

Your humble servant,
Lawrence H. Fairclough.

PS. I should add that Harriet's little hand healed very well; there were no lasting effects. I do not doubt that she scraped it on a stone as she started away in surprise upon seeing her splendid discovery. Truly, in the realm of fairies, children have proved to be our most visionary and bold adventurers!

12th September 1921

Dear Mr Gardner,

It was with great pleasure that I received your letter, with your extremely interesting and exciting news. We were especially delighted that it followed on so quickly from my sending you the approximate copy of my missive to Sir Arthur, who unfortunately has not yet been able to reply, being, as I am sure he is, extremely taken up with the many demands on his time.

But we may be included in a book – and one written by Sir Arthur! That is thrilling indeed. Charlotte in particular could scarcely rein in her astonishment and delight.

Naturally you will wish to view the fairy first, and you are most welcome to do so at any time you require. I am sure you will be satisfied with it. I can only express how pleased I am that Sir Arthur is undeterred by the naysayers all about him and is desirous only of discovering the Truth. In that I shall remain his servant, most particularly so should he ever wish to visit in person. I believe it is laudable to turn the light of scientific enquiry upon what some would describe as an unknowable world, as well as upon that of touchable things. If he could achieve his wishes, and prove the existence of a spiritual realm –! But I shall try to set aside my excitement, and answer the questions you put, before turning to another thrilling matter.

I believe you are quite correct in your supposition that a sunny day is best for catching a sight of the little folk. It was indeed summer, an especially bright day, and almost noon when we had our glimpse; though both of us felt quite well, and there was no question of our being overwhelmed by heat stroke. There was a little haze in the air over the meadows, but once in the glen it was not especially hot, being pleasantly shaded by trees and with the cooling influence of the beck.

It is an interesting notion that 'higher vibrations' may be detected in the noontide shimmer, and indeed that it was some peculiarity of the day or something inherent within ourselves that made us able to see them. It is possible indeed that fairies lie outside our usual visible colour spectrum, though I must say that the little skeleton is quite visible in the shade of our outbuilding, at least with the assistance of my magnifying glass. Do you think there is something special about that lens, and perhaps that of a camera, that has the same effect?

To your next point, however, that we might have glimpsed some 'thought-form', a type of reflection of our innermost imaginings – I think that is what you meant? – I can say that the little body certainly possesses an objective reality, and I am sure when you visit you will come to the same conclusion.

You also posit that the fairies may be from a different branch of evolution from that of humanity, perhaps even springing from the same line as winged insects. Having seen the remains, I consider that rather likely. Indeed, the fragile wings are veined like those of a dragonfly, although the skeleton itself did remind me rather more of a bird. Perhaps they could be related to both somehow, or indeed neither? Without the examination of someone rather more expert in these matters, I doubt we shall be able to hit upon anything conclusive.

In answer to your last point, your certainty that Harriet's tender age and innocence will assist in future sightings is very encouraging. As you say, Elsie and Frances are possibly now too old for such things. I am afraid, however, that the question of whether my granddaughter has some loose-knit ectoplasmic material in her body, giving her a special clairvoyant power, is beyond my ability to ascertain. I am also unsure as to whether the Wright girls' growing up and perhaps even falling in love should entirely end the possibility of their seeing fairies. I saw them myself after all, though no doubt with less clarity than Harriet, whose eyes are younger and sharper. She was certainly the first to notice them and draw my attention to their presence.

I so look forward to being able to discuss these matters in person! Until such time, and spurred onward by your news, I have not rested on my laurels. I rather felt that I should renew my acquaintance with the fairies and attempt to find such evidence of the living beings as I can.

With that in mind, I have several times turned my steps towards Cottingley Beck on my wanderings, and I have often been accompanied by Harriet's mother, who is most intrigued by the whole matter. We have naturally encouraged Harriet to accompany us, being curious as to what she might espy, but we have been a little hampered in this by her own inclinations. I am sorry to report that my granddaughter has taken a sudden aversion to the place. She insists the fairy man stung her, though I am certain I saw no tiny spear or any possible means by which he could have done so. When asked why he would do such a thing, being a dear little creature as he is, she replies only that he did not like being looked at.

Sadly, I have not on any other occasion seen a fairy. Charlotte is the only one among us with anything out of the ordinary to relate.

She was standing apart from us when it happened, as I had taken Harriet to examine some rather fine fungi that had sprung up at the base of a fallen ash tree. We had rather vainly persuaded the child to venture close to the spot of her original sighting, but I am afraid she had closed her eyes tight shut and refused to open them until I led her away.

Charlotte remained by the beck, and I last saw her settling

upon a low branch to better enjoy the cleansing air of the stream, her face dampened by the cold spray. She appeared quite serene, and so I was startled when she began calling my name.

We hurried to her side. I did not like her look; her countenance had paled, whilst her eyes glittered with almost unearthly excitement. For a moment she could not speak, though I kept asking 'What is it?', and Harriet was quite stricken and pulled incessantly on her mother's sleeve.

At length, Charlotte calmed enough to say 'little dancers!' and she pointed at the rock where I had found the fairy body. She went on to explain that she saw lights playing over the water, and thinking them nothing but reflections had, rather dreamily, half closed her eyes, when suddenly she made out a brighter flash among them, in the most exquisite shade of turquoise. That was followed by one in green and another in lilac; and then she saw the swirl of skirts, the gleam of golden hair, and the points of tiny, bird-like eyes, which, she said, were 'quite dark'.

She thought she made out sounds also, as of diminutive pipes, almost beyond the range of her hearing; and said she imagined she could have followed that sound all the way to Fairyland. She did admit later that it might simply have been the sound of birdsong combined with the powers of suggestion, but that is mere supposition.

That was when she had shouted, and the lights vanished at once.

The emotion they engendered was very marked and apparent, however, for when she had finished relating the incident she covered her face and burst into tears. I felt quite overcome myself. I wonder what the feelings of mankind shall be, when all may share in the certainty of the existence of such extraordinary beings! The thrill of it sounds in my blood!

For a full ten minutes, all my daughter-in-law could add was that they were 'so beautiful'. Harriet said nothing; she stood scowling, with her arms crossed over her chest, and refused to look for them at all. And so, after I had cast about and found nothing, we made our way home, where we scarcely knew what to do with ourselves for the wonder of it. I resolved to note it all down in my diary, so that I should forget nothing and could later, if called upon, recount the incident fully; it is by my side as I write.

Harriet watched as I made my record, though she continued rather sulky and refused to comment. She would only say that she thought them ugly, and that they did not truly dance at all; and she would not be drawn further on the subject.

That is the whole of our first-hand experience since my last letter. It is not everything, however, for I have endeavoured to be your faithful assistant and have made visits to certain of our neighbours to ask their views, concentrating particularly on those with young children or who live nearest the glen.

I recognise that the newspapers made assiduous enquiries following the article in *The Strand* which unveiled the photographs, but the villagers here are not the most forthcoming to strangers, and suspicion is easily aroused. Particularly telling, I thought, was their reaction as related in the *Westminster Gazette* this January (yes, I am rather afraid I have seen it). That the local folk dismissed the story as untrue deterred me not at all, since that seemed entirely in character with their bluff way of repelling incomers. Of more interest was the comment that no one else had seen the fairies, but everyone in the village was aware of their supposed existence.

Of course, that could be taken to mean they all knew of the stories put about by Elsie and Frances. But it seemed to me suggestive of some older knowledge, particularly when viewed against their reluctance to speak of such matters, as if some deeper current prevented them.

At any rate, I decided to approach them openly, if not as a local of the requisite number of generations at least as a fellow resident, and ask them directly what I had before only alluded to in our limited conversations. I hoped in this way to overcome any reluctance they may harbour, but I am sorry to say they continued if anything even more recalcitrant. The Wrights would not see me at all, though I suppose I cannot blame them for that. The attention from various newspapers as well as the idle curious and impertinent sceptics must have greatly stretched their patience, and since you have been in regular contact with them yourself, it was scarcely worth placing further pressures upon them.

But I found an equal measure of reluctance throughout the village. Heads were shaken; others laughed; one old gaffer, only slightly more talkative than the rest, told me to my face to 'Have a care'.

Another dame said not a word but left me standing in the doorway whilst she rustled about within. I had begun to doubt whether she intended to return when she appeared again, silent as before, and pressed an old, battered volume into my hand. Then she closed the door in my face. The book was Edwin Sidney Hartland's *The Science of Fairy Tales: an Inquiry into Fairy Mythology*, though it is surely too old to be of much use now. I suppose she was at least trying to be helpful, but there's 'nowt so queer as folk', as they say in these parts.

Needless to add, I shall continue my observations until such time as you can come. To that end, and in emulation of your experiments, I have sent for a camera, having made enquiries for the same type as was used by the Wright girl. The Midg quarter-plate should be here imminently, and I shall keep you apprised of the results; I may only hope to be as fortunate as she.

Again, it is a shame that Sir Arthur is unlikely to be able to see our little elf skeleton in person. My son's wife has a volume she particularly hoped he might sign; but such a great man must be under terrible pressures. We very much anticipate your own visit. To think that you were here in August, and we did not chance to meet! It is a pity that the Wright children had not then the opportunity to get more pictures, as they had the previous summer. As you stated, there was the most dismal rain. And it is true that a small seam of coal has been discovered in the locality, but there is not so very much disruption, I trust, as to prevent our own enquiries.

We shall hope for sunshine, and a steady hand to point the

camera, and the good fortune to choose our moment; and we look forward to welcoming you to Cottingley as early as you are able.

Yours sincerely,
Lawrence H. Fairclough

17th September 1921

Dear Mr Gardner,

I dare say you did not expect another letter so soon after your own, but I could barely contain myself until your visit, which we now anticipate as a fixed event on the 21st. I have news to impart that would not wait, for we have triumphed – I have before me two photographs of the fairies!

I hope I do not delude myself when I say they are far better than any of us could have hoped. Some would say they are more nebulous and uncertain than those of Elsie Wright and Frances Griffiths, but I think in some peculiar way that has become their strength.

In the first you see the stream, with the little rock where I found the body. Do you make out the darting lights before it? Look closely and you will see tiny forms within – there is the merest suggestion of two legs and arms, and the most brilliant points of brightness, you see, are in the form of wings. If you could only see their colours! Perhaps their brilliance is something connected with speed of movement – although then every hummingbird must carry its own halo, so these must be quicker still.

The second shows my dear little Harriet. See how rapt she is about the sprite just approaching her from below! She looks almost afraid. She is a tentative little thing – but her fascination is plain. And the figure is clearer yet than in the first. Indeed, I believe it might even be the same pippin-faced fellow I saw before, though I cannot be certain of identifying individuals from among them. Indeed, I must hold the photograph close to my face to see the detail; I am afraid I have quite belied the spirit of Sherlock Holmes, for I have somehow mislaid my magnifying glass.

Still, I believe I can make out the fairy's form clearly enough, though to be sure, his movement has rendered it a little indistinct. Harriet was rather frozen in place, and so you see quite plainly her fair curls and long-lashed eyes, so like her father's. But you shall see them for yourself, for I am enclosing prints with this letter, along with some photographs I took of the little skeleton. You may imagine how impatient I have been whilst I had them processed – I heard that Mr Wright has a darkroom under the stairs, but I have none, and had to send them out.

I dare say you will find the images of the skeleton the most interesting, not only for their clarity, but for the fact that you will have seen nothing like them in the whole course of your enquiries. I long to hear your response – though I am now caught up entirely in the thought of finding again the living creatures, for how gay and gladsome they look, engaged in their darting and dancing!

What the photographs lack in definition they make up for, I think, in the expression of that movement. Though of course your expert, Snelling, referred to some movement in the Wright photographs, I confess – and I trust you will not be offended – I found it difficult to detect. In these, it is unmistakeable; they are redolent of life.

Another difference is in the size of the little beings. In the previous photographs they appear to be about seventeen or eighteen inches high. Perhaps the girls were fortunate to meet with a higher order of fairy? These are minuscule, but very bright.

It is quite the stir in our household, and we are impatient to share our joy in the matter with the world at large. Do you really think Sir Arthur will be unable to come? Perhaps, with Harriet to accompany him, he might even glimpse the fairies himself! I am certain he would be thrilled by their presence, as we all are.

My daughter-in-law in particular is seized with fairy fervour, and often wends her way down to the glen. I should add that she took the enclosed photographs of the living fairies herself; I would have liked to have done so, but my old legs are less nimble of late, and I often remain at the house to keep company with Harriet whilst her mother plays the detective for all of us.

Alas, I did not see the fairies this time. The descriptions and indeed the photographs are Charlotte's, though the excitement is all my own. It scarcely surpasses hers, in recent days. As I said, she has quite thrown herself into the project. She will sit by the beck for an entire morning or afternoon, staring through the camera lens and waiting for a glimpse; and though the weather is turning rather chill, she says she does not feel it.

She has also taken to borrowing my key to the outhouse, and will stand staring at the little skeleton for hours together. Indeed, she began to worry that something would happen to it, or that it might be 'stolen away'. I am sure, having kept silence on its existence with all outside the family save yourself and Sir Arthur, it is safe enough, but she persuaded me to take it into the house. She placed the box under her bed herself, and says its presence is a great relief to her.

To be entirely open and honest, I am somewhat relieved that she no longer feels the need to constantly open the box and gaze at the skeleton. I have done so only once, to take its photograph. Is it not a peculiar object? The decay has progressed no further, and it remains quite intact, as you will see.

But soon you may examine it for yourself. I anticipate the day. We shall not cease until then to obtain further evidence, but I am certain we already possess such that the world will fall before all your arguments. It will be, as Sir Arthur so eloquently put it in his momentous article in *The Strand*, an epoch-making revelation.

Sincerely yours,
Lawrence H. Fairclough.

PS. It is interesting you say in your last letter that Elsie Wright also referred to the fairies being ugly, though it seems she witnessed some kind of transformation from beauty to ugliness all in an instant. I wonder if Harriet saw some such thing, but was a little slower in observing the process of change? It is hard to imagine such beauty dissolving to its opposite. But good and evil exists in all men, so perhaps it is concentrated too in these little beings. And how much better to wear the honest semblance of inner thoughts and feelings on the outside, rather than hiding them within!

Perhaps she merely saw some little aversion to our disruption of their lives, which would seem reasonable enough, since we were present at the passing of the tiny maid, or at least shortly after. That would explain, I suppose, how beauteous Charlotte has thought them since – they have perhaps forgotten all, as the mayfly forgets its mortality and flits gladsome in the sunshine, and are quite restored.

Charges to pay

s._____ d.

RECEIVED

POST  OFFICE

TELEGRAM

Prefix   Time handed in.   Office of Origin and Service Instructions.   Words.

From   Orig: Bradford, United Kingdom   8. 54 PM

LONDON TELEGRAPH OFFICE, 19 SEPTEMBER 1921

MR E L GARDNER
MUST CANCEL VISIT –(STOP)– APOLOGIES FOR
BREVITY AND INCONVENIENCE –(STOP)– STRUCK BY
SEVEREST MISFORTUNE –(STOP)– LETTER TO
FOLLOW WHEN ABLE

MR L H FAIRCLOUGH

For free repetition of doubtful words call, with this form at office of delivery. Other enquiries should be accompanied by this form and if possible, the envelope

20th September 1921

Dear Mr Gardner,

I scarcely know how to begin. First, may I extend my deepest apologies for having to defer your visit. Please rest assured that we had anticipated it most particularly and would only ever have done so in the direst circumstance. There was certainly no rudeness intended; indeed, I am mortified to imagine what you must think. I trust, when I explain all, you will understand.

We have been struck by misfortune, not upon one count, but two. I shall begin, I suppose, and treat them chronologically, if not by the import with which we are affected.

First, the little skeleton you so particularly wished to see is gone. I do not know wither or how, but I feel its loss most acutely, or did so until worse came to take its place. I discovered its absence myself. I cannot express to you my astonishment and distress. Indeed, my pulse became so rapid I feared the worst; it took some moments to compose myself enough to peer once more under Charlotte's bed.

I do not know what had carried me into the room to look at the skeleton – I suppose with your arrival growing imminent, I wished to be certain that all was prepared to your liking. And yet the box was not there, and I thought my old heart would burst at last.

I do not know how my daughter-in-law had not noticed the lack. She had been so assiduous in watching over the box. I could not think what had happened, unless she had decided its hiding place too precarious after all, and had found another. I comforted myself with that as best I could. She was then in the kitchen and I hastened to ask her, though I could hardly form the words. I saw at once it was no use. Her eyes opened wide with surprise, and I cannot adequately explain, but I *felt* the lack of it – that the fairy had blessed us with its presence, and had now gone from us, and would remain far beyond our reach.

I think I must have had a little turn, for Charlotte assisted me to a chair and helped me recover myself. I kept asking after the box, pushing aside the glass of water she held to my lips. I wanted nothing – only that which has become so precious to all of us! And she kept shaking her head and looking so sad – her eyes filled with tears, as much with dismay at my wildness as at the loss, I think. But we had also roused Harriet from her accustomed place in the nursery. She delights at that time in sitting in the window seat deeply lost in a book, but I realised she was standing by me, quite stricken.

I endeavoured to compose myself, but my distress overcame my sense, for the only words I said were, 'Did you take it, Harriet – did you wish to play with the little maid under the bed?'

I saw at once from her expression that not only was she thoroughly upset by the imputation but she found the idea abhorrent, as of course it should have been. What child plays with a skeleton?

Her demeanour at least had the effect of bringing me around and returning me to a care for those whom I love, at the expense of all the world and its beliefs and its knowledge. I comforted her, and in doing so in some measure comforted myself, though it sickens me to write of it still. I do believe I would grieve the creature as a human friend, if it were not that further misfortune has taken its place in all our hearts.

Although I was in some wise resolved to face the loss, and the possibility that it would expose me to censure from yourself and the great man we admire so well, my daughter-in-law could not allow it to rest. I curse myself for it! For it was in part her concern for me that must have driven her to put on her mackintosh and go to seek the little thing at once. Yet, I do not believe that to be the whole of it. I have previously mentioned her fascination; the little form always had exerted some pull over her.

Charlotte at once imagined, not that some thief had stolen it away, but that the fairy had somehow been returned to the glen. I am not sure why she thought so. Perhaps she caught the idea from me that it had gone beyond us, to some world that we could not reach after – but she did reach after it. I would that she had not!

She insisted, however, and to my great shame I did not press her to stay, for she raised some hope in me that all would be well. Perhaps she would find the skeleton lying on the rocks, or in some leafy bower – and so I let her go, and even wished her luck. I stood with Harriet and watched her hurrying away without so much as looking back, so intent was she upon her quest.

I sat with the child and leafed over her book with her (it was the Brothers Grimm, though I cringed inwardly to see it), and ruffled her curls – as much to reassure myself, I think, as her. Time passed. The grandfather clock marked out the minutes with its mellow ticking, and the chime marked the quarter hour and then the half, and then the hour. I realised we were no longer looking at the book. Harriet sat quite still, a pensive expression on her face, her lower lip pinched between her teeth. I stared out of the window, though all was a-blur, and I do not think I had been conscious of gazing at anything.

I examined the clock once more and found that another hour had begun. I stood and I paced. I prepared bread and butter for Harriet and she picked at it; I could eat none. We waited, and after a time Harriet went to her room. She slept, I think, or curled up on her bed and tried to.

The afternoon was fading towards evening. The days are growing short, and shadows were stretching and joining without.

My unease grew. For I could not help but think of what Charlotte had said once, about following the sound of magical pipes all the way to Fairyland. I had lost my wife and my son, and could not bear the idea of Charlotte being lost to me too, following some fairy dance to a place where she could never again be reunited with Harry – my boy!

Grief overcame me. I did not put on my coat but rushed out as I was and started towards the beck.

As I went I thought I discerned a darker shape at the edge of the verdure where the trees began. At first it blended into the gloaming, visible only by its odd and rather irregular movement. It was not like a man, nor any animal I had hitherto seen. The figure almost appeared to lurch along, feeling its way, and I hurried towards it, already feeling the presentiment of some dreadful tragedy. With equal parts relief and dismay, I saw as I grew closer that it was Charlotte. She was stumbling along with one arm outstretched, and the other clamped to her left eye.

I did not call out as I ran to her; I wanted only to reach her as quickly as I could. She looked up, staring at me with her one eye, and so it startled me beyond measure when I grasped her arms and she screamed in sudden terror. I cried out, calling her name, and I tried to pull her hand from her face. I wanted to see what was the matter, but she drew back from me. 'I'm blind,' she said. 'Blind!'

I cannot describe my horror. I have not the powers of a Conan Doyle or other great writer. My head swam, but she implored me to help her to the house, and so I did; I supported her and guided her. I did not understand. She had covered only one eye; surely she could see her way with the other? But from her hesitant steps and half-muted sounds of distress, it seemed she could not.

I could not fathom what had happened, or how such horror had visited her in such a lovely place, with such lovely creatures in it. What did it mean?

She spoke little that night. I gave her a measure of brandy, which quieted her, and I settled her on the sofa since she was unwilling to move; but she did at last uncover her left eye. I had dreaded what I might see, but it appeared normal, to my great relief. She only murmured one thing to me as she succumbed to the draught and fell into a doze.

'They spit in your eye,' she said. 'They spit in your eye, and it's gone. If I had not covered the other –'

She was blind, you see, but not in the eye she had covered. She had lost the sight in her right eye and had kept her hand over her left to protect it from them. I know not how such a thing could happen, or if she had become confused somehow about the cause and had mistaken the little creatures' intentions. I hardly dare to speculate, but something is terribly wrong.

I will try to write again soon.

Yours most sincerely,
Lawrence Fairclough.

24th September 1921

Dear Mr Gardner,

Thank you for your letter, and indeed your good wishes. It is a salve to my heart on one count at least, that you do not think badly of us for so precipitately deferring your visit.

I shall take up where I left off: with the question of Charlotte's sight. It is indeed the presiding concern of our household. Her right eye remains dark, and it is doubly unfortunate for she says her left eye has always been the weaker, and so she has not only a shadow over all she sees, but everything is less distinct than before.

I have tried, quietly and gently, to speak to her of what happened, but she will not be drawn on it; save for one thing, to which I will return.

I took her to Bradford to have her examined by an ophthalmologist. He could see nothing wrong and suggested a kind of hysterical blindness brought on by extreme anxiety. I wonder if this is so. I hardly dare believe, for if that is the case her sight may be restored naturally. He said she would gradually see lights – but she shuddered at that, and he did not go on.

Indeed, the three of us pass our days sunk into gloom, for though I almost allow myself to hope for recovery, Charlotte is adamant it will not occur; and thus far bitter experience has proved her correct.

Charlotte is resilient under her suffering, however. If I try to discuss it with her, or even if she catches me watching her, she smiles as if she is the one who needs to reassure me. She said to me once, the key of her voice soft and low, that there are 'worse things in the world,' and I knew that she was thinking of the loss of my son. How brave she is! He would have been proud of her forbearance. And at least she can still see little Harriet's face – I know she takes comfort in that. More than ever before, she likes nothing so much as to have the child sit on her knee, and to rest her cheek against her golden curls. Such a wistful look comes across her face then – ah, but it is full of love as well as sorrow, and the former, I must believe, shall always triumph over the latter.

It heals my own heart to see them so, which is of inestimable relief because I have worried incessantly. Charlotte does not wish to speak of the fairies, as I have stated; and I have said little of them, other than to press upon her that she must never return to the glen. If something else were to befall her…How much more terrible would it be for something to happen to her good eye? How dreadful, to be cast altogether into the dark! And she says she will not go, but there is a terrible restlessness in her. I sense it beneath the surface, even when she sits over her sewing, tilting her head to see it the better.

I should return, now, to the single occasion when Charlotte has spoken to me of the fairies. It was late one evening, when I had, as is the way of old men, nodded off before the fire. Charlotte had retired some time before, and Harriet of course had been long abed. It must have been late because the fire was reduced to only a few fitful embers, now setting the room agleam, now plunging all into darkness. Somewhere without, an owl hooted mournfully about the house.

I did not trouble with a lamp; I knew my way well enough. I went up the stairs, making sure not to knock the treads and make a noise about it. I did not wish to wake anyone, but it seemed someone was awake after all, for as I reached the passage the door halfway along it opened.

It was the door to Charlotte's room. I went towards it, and when I reached the opening I realised she was standing there, quite silently, staring out. Both her eyes were unblinking and fixed; none could have said that one of them was blank.

I began to apologise. I thought I must have frightened her, that she had heard some sound after all and was looking out in terror of what might have come for her. But she leaned out and thrust something towards me. I closed my hand upon it; I did not at first recognise what it was.

'I saw them.' She spoke in a low voice, little more than a whisper, and yet it was full of a hoarse wildness. 'They took her back. I witnessed their solemnities.'

I opened my mouth to question her, to calm her, but she stepped back and closed the door in my face. I stared at it; I thought I heard a bedspring settling. I decided the best course was to leave her. I went to my room and lit the lamp at my bedside. It was only then that I made out what she had given me: the little cloth-bound volume, *The Science of Fairy Tales: an Inquiry into Fairy Mythology*. I had not even known she was reading it.

I leafed through the book before I slept, finding within a peculiar mixture of curiosities. Some was obviously fiction, some intended to be fact, and some consisting of rather fantastical conclusions. Indeed, it should not have surprised me to discover a chapter headed 'Savage Ideas'.

I did not examine the book again until the morning. I slept ill – I think the odd thoughts it conjured had followed me into sleep. Still, I opened it the next day and confirmed my night-time impression of there being some very strange matter within. Have you read it? I wish I could ask directly – but no mind. I shall relate some of the phantasmagoria which passed before my eyes.

There are stories of midwives summoned to mansions filled with singing and dancing, to ease a fairy birth; others of the perils of eating fairy food, lest travellers in their realms become trapped there for ever; and tales of terrible revenge for some accidental slight. Still more tell of changelings – children or adults carried away into Fairyland, replaced by worn-out fairies or stocks of wood bewitched to resemble the stolen person. And there are stories that speak of the fairies' dislike of being observed, and of their various retaliations.

And here is the point. Sometimes the person prying is magically deprived of their sight; sometimes the fairy plucks out their eye or pokes it out with a stick; others blow a mysterious powder into the face. Sometimes, however, that aim is accomplished by the fairy spitting in their eye. 'All water is wine,' they have been reported to say, 'and thy two eyes are mine!'

Whatever the means, it all has the same awful effect: the unfortunate person can see no more.

You will see why I do not know what to think. Surely such benevolent creatures as we have seen would do no such thing. And what of Elsie Wright? She claims to have often seen and played with them in the fairy glen. I wonder: why did such never happen to her?

But the same book tells me that fairies can choose to manifest themselves to humans. It is where people spy upon their private affairs that objection is encountered, and perhaps that is what we did, upon seeing the little dead body. I would that I had never taken the thing! It is possible that we have been punished – though the curse has not fallen to me or Harriet, but her mother.

Despite all, I continue to feel the loss of the little skeleton. It is like a constant ache. I wonder and wonder what became of it. We three – and you – are the only ones to know of its existence. And I think of the words that Charlotte whispered to me in the dark: *They took her back.*

Perhaps the fairies did indeed break their bounds and trespass into the human world, and came for her; and yet, if so, the time of reclaiming the little maid is precisely when they have chosen to deal out such terrible punishment for her loss.

There is an image I carry in my mind – the prone body in the midst of all her fellows, moving in stately array in whatever rites and 'solemnities' they may possess. Perhaps they have ushered her into the next world – or welcomed her into their own again.

On a smaller matter, I am reminded that some odd happenings about the house could almost make me believe we are subject to some continuing fairy mischief. With more momentous issues to face, I had rather put them from my mind until this moment. You will notice, for example, that my letter is rather disfigured with blots. I have had much cause for my hand to shake, but I do not believe it to have done so to excess, and yet the ink constantly drips about. It is a disgrace next to your own type-written communications, and I cannot account for it at all.

My magnifying glass continues to be mysteriously vanished, as are a few other sundry items; flour is constantly spilt about the kitchen; and the milk rapidly turns sour, although it has not been left out and the days have not been so very warm.

But these small inconveniences might somehow be the result of Charlotte's poor sight, and the anxious condition of her mind that must necessarily follow; and I can only apologise if my old hands are in a more agitated state of vexation than I am fully conscious of.

It only remains to sign myself,

Very sincerely yours,
Lawrence Fairclough.

28th September 1921

Dear Mr Gardner,

Thank you for your last. Yes, we continue as well as could be
anticipated, although in spite of all our wishes the sight in
Charlotte's right eye has not returned.

I have considered very carefully your suggestion that my
daughter-in-law may have taken some hint from Mr Hartland's
book. I suppose it is possible that some fancy has taken hold of
her, resulting in a real impediment to her vision. It is another
example of the perennial question: which came first, the chicken
or the egg.

After much thought, I rather decided it was beside the point.
There is much supposition in these parts and beyond that fairies
are the mere invention of children, yet I have held the little skeleton
in my own hand, and felt its weightlessness. I cannot doubt them
to be real and, that being so, what other mysteries may exist?

The only point at question, then, is whether they are wicked
and vengeful or innocent of wrongdoing. I would wish to hope –
being part of God's creation, as I like to assume – they are blithe
and good and mean us only well, but I wonder. Indeed, Hartland's
book describes beings that are not purely benevolent but

composed of 'caprice and vindictiveness, if not cruelty.' But how would he know? Perhaps they are neither good nor bad, being of some alternative line of evolution as you have proposed, and have no more morality than does an insect or a bird.

On another point, I can assure you that Charlotte's blindness is quite genuine. In order to do so, I have been sure to watch her carefully. Her eye looks perfectly normal, but I have many times seen her tilt her head and squint to see better with her one good eye, or to reach for some object and misjudge its distance without the aid of the other. If this is a pretence, it is a good one; and really, I cannot suspect her of any deception. She is of a steady, upright, honest, sober character, and I know if you saw her and conversed with her that you could not consider there was any trickery involved.

You mention that if there is no possibility of human falsity, you would be pleased to re-arrange your visit. You ask if you may speak to her and examine her eye. She would pass any test, I am certain of that, but she remains reluctant to speak of the little folk or even hear anything said about them. She has undergone a dreadful experience, and I cannot at present subject her to such an ordeal. Perhaps a few more weeks will see her settled enough to consider the matter again. I am sure the results would be worthy of your patience. Though it strikes me that Sir Arthur is a trained ophthalmologist, is he not? If there were any medical advantage that may be gained, I could try to impress upon her the importance of a visit from you both. I am sure the thrill of meeting such a personage would outweigh any difficulty.

But we do continue a trifle unsettled. I have mentioned before some small incidents that, whilst of a mere domestic sphere, are really rather inconvenient. They have not ceased; if anything, they have worsened since my last. Charlotte cannot set down her needle without it seemingly vanishing into the air, and neither can she sew for pricking her fingers. Harriet constantly complains that her books have been moved or her pages lost, even torn out. I know that some would raise their eyebrows and blame the child for the mischief but, really, she has never been prone to naughtiness. Besides which, she treasures her books, and I am sure she would do no such thing to any in her possession.

The dinner is often spoiled. Charlotte says the range can no longer be trusted. Sometimes it will not boil a kettle; at other times it will not draw and chokes us all with smoke. The smuts go everywhere, blackening our clothing and the walls. One can even taste it in our bread. It is most unpleasant. I see Harriet pulling faces over it, though bless the child, she eats it anyway, casting glances about the room as if concerned who might be watching.

Of course, all such things are explainable. I do not claim any particular supernatural agency; I have no reason to believe it to be the folk. And yet I wonder; and I have cause, as I will relate.

It is strange to say, after everything that has passed, that Harriet has begun to speak to me of returning to the glen. This very much surprised me at first, and I did not like to re-awaken her fears by questioning the wisdom of it, but I did ask whether she very much wished to go.

'Oh yes,' she said, 'I think we must, for Mama's sake.'

I did not like to probe her meaning. I suppose she wished to show her parent she was not afraid, but then she said, 'We need to stop them from being angry about the house.'

I gathered myself to respond, but she added, 'They don't really like us. They don't want to play. They don't really know how to dance. They only wish to make us want to be where they are.'

'And where is that, child?' I asked, but she would not say, or indeed utter another word. She continued pensive all that afternoon, as if afraid of having said too much.

I cannot help thinking of Elsie and Frances, who loved to 'tice' the fairies and played so gaily among them, just as one imagines children doing. But Harriet has always been such a funny little thing; she prefers her books to the company of others, and then, she has found no suitable playmate. If I had not seen the fairies myself I could easily imagine her to have invented little companions to meet the deficiency.

Alison Littlewood

Such is all my news. It remains only to sign myself,

Yours sincerely,
Lawrence Fairclough.

30th September 1921

Dear Mr Gardner,

You will no doubt be surprised to hear from me so soon after my last, and without awaiting a reply in the interim. I shall tell you the reason at once.

I fell into rather a reverie yester-evening, and began thinking again of Elsie and Frances and their gladsome encounter with Fairyland, which seemed to bring them nothing but joy; and I contrasted it with our own household, fallen so deeply into a constant anxious silence.

And I thought how odd it was – now I must apologise, Mr Gardner, and trust you will not think me impertinent, but I only wish to express honestly what I felt – that Charlotte's photographs appeared so much more realistic than those published in *The Strand*.

I always thought they appeared rather flat, you see. I know that people wiser than I had examined them and detected signs that the fairies were moving, even your expert in photographic fakery, and yet I never could see it, not really. I blame my old eyes and my ignorance, of course; I am perfectly happy to be guided by wiser men than I. Indeed, I understand you to be the reference for lantern slides and images for the Theosophical Society, but I always somehow felt they had rather a cardboard cut-out quality that did not sit well with the living child next to them.

Then I thought of the missing skeleton, the incontrovertible proof that was so much needed, and I suddenly much desired to look upon our own photographs again.

I opened the bureau and took out the envelope. They had not disappeared; the plates are still in my keeping. I have checked them all several times and nothing has vanished, but despite that, something within them seems sadly changed.

The little living lights I had seen previously, with the suggestion of limbs and the bright haloes made by their wings, appear to have faded. Arms and legs are turned to clumsy lines; the motion of the wings no longer obscures their ornamented shapes, which I think look nothing like those of the fairy I held in my hands. Their hair almost appears coiffed, like that of the Wright girl's rather Parisienne styled maids; and their dresses, now quite distinct, are as frilled and quilled as any lady's in a ballroom.

I have not ceased to be puzzled by the change. They no longer appear to be in motion but are sharply frozen; indeed, the little fellow pictured with Harriet is now more distinct than she. I cannot account for it at all. Have my eyes deceived me – were they always so?

I wished to ask Charlotte, but she refused to look at them, and it would be unfair to upset Harriet by pressing her. Instead my thoughts turned to you, and what you would think of it – what anyone would think.

You are in possession of copies of the earlier pictures, but how may we compare? Perhaps they never appeared to you as they did to me. Perhaps you thought me mad from the beginning and only humour what you see as the fancies of an old man. Pray tell me honestly what you think of them. I can only hope that yours continue as they once appeared, or you shall think me the most terrible confidence man – nothing but a trickster, when it is not I – but they! For the fairies must have changed them somehow, just as they have changed my home and my family; just as they adorn my words with ugly drips of ink; as they have changed everything.

In truth, I would that I had never seen them. I would that

Harriet had not gone poking into the hollows with her stick. I would that I had never come to Cottingley!

I anticipate your reply, in rather a state of agitation.

Most sincerely yours,
Lawrence Fairclough.

5th October 1921

Dear Mr Gardner,

Thank you for your letter. It is true that it is very difficult to compare in writing one's impressions of photographs. To judge by your description, the fairies have remained in position, and yet I rather fear they have flattened somehow – that they are not so redolent of life as I felt they were.

But it is impossible to draw any conclusions without *seeing*. I do not know if they now appear quite dead, and you are being tactful; if they have become more like the Wright photographs, which have at least been accepted by experts; or if they remain as they once were.

I am considering going to the glen to get more pictures. At least then we should have some other point of comparison, but if the same thing happened again I think I might despair. What can one do against such subterfuge? And it is all around me... it is becoming difficult to consume a meal in our own home for the cheese being mouldy or the meat maggoty. Against all our preferences, we are driven out to eat. Indeed, I wonder if we may be driven out altogether.

I long to be a thousand miles from any mention of the word

fairy, and yet I cannot escape it; it is in Harriet's pensive expression, constantly looking at me as if to say, 'Shall we go?', and in Charlotte's look of gentle sorrow as she bends closely over her work.

I have even begun to dream of them. They visit me each night in the darkest hours, and each time I am taken in, because the dream begins with my waking. I hear them first. There are words I cannot make out, spoken in mellifluous tones followed by tinklings of silver laughter, and there is more of the clicking I heard by the stream. I open my eyes expecting to see them dancing in the air, and I do, but I am surprised at their proximity; the little green fellow is leaning right over me. I catch one glimpse of his tiny features before he reaches out, quicksilver fast, and all goes black.

I try to open my eyes again. I bat my hands before my face, afraid of what the fairies are doing; my hands close on nothing. I try to open my eyes and see only the dark.

I reach up, feeling my own eyelids, dragging them upward. It is difficult to tell but I think they are already open. And that is when I wake, when the first terror of it closes upon me.

But it is only a dream; and many would doubtless claim that I have spent far too long lending such things credence already. And as you said, Charlotte's condition may well be the result of suggestion – of, ironically, prying too far into the mysteries, upsetting the balance of her mind to the degree that she is physically affected.

I shall endeavour to learn from the spirit of Sherlock Holmes, and take a more scientific approach.

It is difficult to do, however, whilst living in such a place. Indeed, I have further reason to think it benighted – but I shall explain. Driven, as I said, for want of unspoiled food, we have taken dinner in the parlour of a local hostelry. It was not the first time we had been forced to do so, and the novelty of it was somewhat tarnished; we spoke little, until the landlady came in and asked how we did.

We responded with the usual pleasantries. And then Harriet

held up her glass of milk and said, 'The fairies don't like this. It's the special milk they want.'

The lady replied as one would expect, in the tones of humouring a child; and we went on quite dully until the end of our repast, when she bustled in with a little jug, which she set before the child.

'Beastlings,' she said with a wink. 'That's what the fairies like.'

My daughter-in-law looked up with some annoyance. I think we would have sent the stuff away, but Harriet seized the jug with such eagerness her mother could not have taken it from her. Indeed, the child appeared quite desperate at the idea of its loss, and although I felt considerable dismay at the woman's foolish meddling, I could not bear to remove it either.

Beastlings. It is the word for the first milk after a cow has calved, I believe; it has a peculiarly rich smell and an almost green tinge. I cannot say I altogether like it, and would not bring myself to taste it for the world. But then, that would have upset Harriet too much. She carried it home with the greatest care, and I believe would have gone running to the glen at once had I not told her it must be kept for the morrow.

I could not think what else to do; but I cannot imagine what possessed me to speak those words. For now she expects to go, and I do not know what I shall say to put the light of it out of her eyes.

Yours sincerely,
Lawrence Fairclough.

6th October 1921

Dear Mr Gardner,

Forgive the rather untidy state of my letter. I have news to impart, and write in a state of some excitement.

Only a short time has passed since the worried-over visit to the glen. Harriet awoke full of fervent emotion and brimming with its importance; and to deny her – well, I could not do so, though I would never have gone there again under any other compulsion. Harriet ran and seized her jug of green milk. And then she said her mother must come too.

Well, here was a difficulty. I said we must go alone and that I could not prevail upon her mother for anything; and Harriet behaved most unlike herself, and stamped, and shouted, and wailed; and her mother came all a-flurry to see what was amiss.

Harriet would not be quieted. She said her mother must and should go, and Charlotte only looked grave, and shuddered as if she were suddenly cold. I must confess that her reluctance spread itself to me; all I could think of was my dream, and that glimpse of an impish face before all went dark.

Then an idea struck me. Charlotte had said she was blinded when a fairy spat in her eye. What if she went to the glen, but kept her good eye covered somehow? I made the suggestion and Harriet fell silent at last, her face all raptness and hope.

Charlotte closed both her eyes. Then she rose and left the room.

Harriet and I looked at each other. We did not know if her mother would return, but after a few minutes she did; and she was dressed as I had never thought to see her again. For she had found her widow's bonnet with its finely-meshed veil, the one she had worn when my son was lost to us.

I could not speak. I might have been transported back in time, to the very moment of opening the telegram with shaking hands – it had been sent to Charlotte, but she had been unable to look at it. It was I who had to break the news.

'I think *he* will protect me from them,' she said simply, and began to put on her coat. And then she stopped and said, 'But it is not I who should wear this – it is Harriet!'

I put out a hand to stop her. She made a good point of course, but the idea of the child being dressed in such a thing – it seemed an abomination.

Harriet stepped back and said, 'But I shall wear my hat with the low brim. And I will not let go of Grandpapa's hand.'

As if to demonstrate, she came to my side. Clutching the jug with one hand, she took mine in the other; and I thought at once of some little creature coming and spitting in her eyes, and her unable to throw up either hand to shield them.

At length, I prevailed upon her to allow me to carry the jug and she reluctantly relinquished it, leaving her one hand free. Then we made to set out, but not without a last delay, for Charlotte stopped at the threshold and would not go on.

Then she said, 'Thus I took the little skeleton. They were supposed to let me in – but it did not happen.'

I could not see her face. I am not sure I could have looked into her eyes if it had been possible. I remained there fixed to the spot and unable to reply, and then she trembled and stepped out.

You may imagine my feelings. All the horror I had

experienced at the loss of the skeleton was before me again – and here was the cause: not a fairy, but the woman who stood to me as a daughter. How could she do it? But the *why* soon came to outweigh the *how*. For what must her feelings have been, to do such a thing? Had the fairies gained a hold over her somehow? I remembered the way she had used to hold the box in her hand and stare into it, as if fascinated. Was it only that she wished for nothing more than to go into Fairyland with them, that unknown and perhaps unknowable place? Now we were going straight to them, and holding another gift. Only think what had been her reward before!

Little wonder, then, that she had hesitated. Yet now she strode out boldly, as if to leave us behind. Harriet and I hurried after her. A thousand words crowded my mind, all the things I wanted to say to her mother; but I could not challenge her in front of the child, and we were already committed, and a part of me wished to know what would happen. My curiosity had been roused by the whole affair, and whilst I had come to long for the end of it, I somehow felt that the time was not yet.

Harriet was as good as her word and did not let go of my hand. I was glad, as we went, that my own eye-glasses were in place. Blindness is perhaps the province of the old rather than the young, but believe me when I say that nobody is ever ready for *that*.

As we went the sun was shut out by dense clouds which admitted no glimpse of sky. It was not a bright day and soon it was darker yet for we stepped under the trees, Charlotte still walking ahead of us. She had not once looked back. Harriet and I had not exchanged a word. I felt her fingers close more tightly upon mine as we passed into the deeper shadow.

I was surprised by how far autumn had progressed. It was not that there was anything unusual for the time of year, but I realised I had passed much of the last days ensconced inside. Now the air was cold and crisp, but with nothing enlivening in it. Everything was damp, but diminished; the beck had shrunk to a dull trickle. Leaves of russet and brown speckled the earth but all looked limp and rather dismal and it felt that way, too; there was a dead note to the place. It did not at all feel as when I had last seen it, and I wondered if that was because the fairies had gone.

The idea brought with it an odd sense of loss as well as relief. For they *were* a miracle, were they not? One such as man could marvel over for years to come. And I had seen them, but for everything I had grasped at, I had nothing to show. It reminded me suddenly of the tales I had read in Hartland's book, of fairy gold that turns to nothing but coal when spied upon too greedily.

Charlotte had continued on, and I still could not see her face. I suddenly wished to do so. I called to her and she halted, her head inclined as if focused upon the stream.

'Charlotte, perhaps you should cover your good eye,' I said. 'Here must do, I think.' I made to squeeze Harriet's hand just as her fingers slipped from my own. I started, but she was at my side just as ever; she smiled as if in full agreement, and reached for the jug.

I peered into it with distaste, but I could no longer detect the greenish scent; it was lost in the tang of the stream that hung in the air all around us. I gave it to her. I wanted to clasp my hands over Harriet's eyes but she nodded at me so gravely, as if this is what must be, as if she saw everything –

She turned to the stream, where it fell into the little pool with a dull sound, and no birds sang, and no lights danced about her, and no words were spoken. I heard her breathy intake of air. And she held it high and, as if in a story, tapped her heels together. Then she held the jug over the stream and poured out the contents.

'The milk is free,' she said at last. 'And all shall see!'

I did not know where she had learned the words. The fluid whirled into the eddy, turning it cloudy for an instant, and was gone. Harriet watched, her rosebud lips almost forming a smile. I nodded to suggest that we had finished and may leave, but her expression did not change.

'All done,' I said, my voice falsely bright, and I turned to where Charlotte had been standing. She was not there.

'Mama!' Harriet had seen it too, for her voice lifted in sudden panic. She scrambled past me. I reached for her shoulder and felt it beneath my fingers; then she was running away. Too slow – is that not the way of the old? Too slow and too foolish.

She rushed into the trees. I caught glimpses of her pale dress and flying hair, and then she stopped, because a figure stepped from behind a willow and leaned down and wrapped its arms about her.

It was dark, the figure, half drowned in shadow, and I opened my mouth to call out; then I saw it was only Charlotte, holding her bonnet, and I heard her say Harriet's name in delight.

Harriet froze. Then she squealed and threw her arms about her mother. Both turned and walked towards me, hand in hand, no sign of fear or concern on their faces; and something about Charlotte's expression was different.

'I can see,' she said, her voice full of gladness. 'I see everything!' She opened and closed both eyes as if she could show me, and I think I only looked confused. How could anything have changed so quickly? This was too much, and too soon. It had been too easy. Were the fairies so grateful for a little milk they would bestow such a blessing so simply?

But Charlotte's joy was contagious, creeping from her to me, and she caught my hand in her younger, stronger fingers, and squeezed it. She gave me such a wide smile I could not help smiling back.

'Is it true?' I peered at her more closely. Her eyes appeared just as they had before.

She did not answer: she only laughed.

'I want to go home,' Harriet said, reaching out for me.

I took her warm fingers in mine, but it was Charlotte who spoke. 'Yes,' she said, 'home,' and we turned towards the house, accompanied by the sound of the beck, Charlotte's footsteps following behind our own as Harriet skipped at my side.

So great a blessing, for so small a thing – but perhaps it wasn't so small a thing. Perhaps the fairies saw our offering as an apology.

Perhaps they saw it as a promise; or perhaps there had been no fairies, and I was only an old fool. Charlotte really might have been struck by hysteria, and it was only a belief in her daughter's actions that had released her from whatever spell she had placed over her own mind.

Relief came over me at last. She had her sight – and if there were fairies, they were good after all! It might have been a mistake: they never meant to harm Charlotte's eye. They did not mean to sting Harriet's finger. And yet it felt too easy, too neat; almost as if some trick had been played upon me.

Harriet remained quiet all the way home. She smiled secret smiles to herself, of relief, no doubt. Charlotte kept silence too, overwhelmed perhaps by her own good fortune and the sight of her child, made distinct once more, and without any shadow across it.

It only struck me afterwards that I might have taken the camera. I had quite forgotten my resolve to get more pictures. Perhaps it is just as well. In all honesty, now that we are home together and safe, I hope that we might be done with the whole thing. I remain your humble servant and will answer any questions you require of me, of course, but I think my role as an amateur detective in this matter, such as it was, may well be behind me. I hope you will not mind it, after everything that has befallen us.

Yours sincerely,
Lawrence Fairclough.

4th April 1922

Dear Mr Gardner,

You will perhaps be surprised to hear from me. It has been some few months to be sure, and yet you cannot doubt my continued interest in this affair, no matter my recent silence. I have answered certain small queries you have sent; I hope I have never failed you in that regard. And yet it is with the greatest sense of disappointment that I take up my pen.

I recently obtained a copy of Mr Conan Doyle's book. Indeed, I have awaited *The Coming of the Fairies* with the keenest anticipation, as you may well imagine. You kindly informed me that a significant portion of the account would be taken up with further sightings and evidence of fairies, brought to light after the photographs taken in 1917 and the article in *The Strand* of 1920, and I did not deceive myself, I think, in expecting that my own was to be among them.

Imagine my feelings then, in leafing through it – and again, and indeed again – and finding nothing more than the same scant cases that were the subject of the secondary article in *The Strand* of last March.

I should say, I have no wish to convey my immediate

impressions. My emotions ran very high; and thus I did not write at once. Yet my feelings remain much as they were, albeit a little tempered with time.

The prime cause of my concern, needless to say, is that Sir Arthur may have disregarded my story because he believes it to be a fraud or imposture. Does he class us with the cases that were 'more or less ingenious practical jokes'? Has he truly dismissed us as such? I ask you directly, and I believe, after all my openness upon the matter, I am entitled to do so. Does he consider me a liar and a cheat?

But he can have no doubt, his own belief being what it is! He has many times stood accused of the most dreadful species of foolishness, if not mendacity, and it is difficult to countenance that being his first response to me.

I am a man of honour, Mr Gardner. I have always conducted myself as respectable in business and of decent character in all aspects of my life. I would challenge anyone to find a soul that would not speak for me in that regard. I have invented nothing. I can only mourn such proofs as I have held in my hand and that have gone from me, since they would have made my position unassailable and above reproach.

I have seen fairies. My daughter-in-law has been cruelly blighted for spying upon them and has been restored by their agency. I have held pictures of them in my hand. I have touched their earthly remains. Such is my testimony, stronger than many that are instanced in Sir Arthur's book, and yet my name is struck from the record as surely as if I had never existed.

It cannot be only because he has not made my acquaintance. He never saw Elsie Wright or Frances Griffiths, but has taken the word of others as to the unlikelihood of their having invented anything. He stakes his entire reputation on their photographs being genuine. And yet how great an argument in his favour would it be to show *other* photographs, captured in the same place but at different times and by different hands? It would reaffirm the existence of the sprites – demonstrating, at once and for ever, that theirs was no isolated case.

I know that through some misfortune my photographs had been rendered flattened and dull and without the traces of life they once held, but could they be entirely without purpose? For the ones printed in the book were no great demonstrations, as is evidenced by the public doubt and incomprehension that has greeted them.

Why, even within the text there was some little excuse made for them by an interested party, namely, that the fairies' whiteness was the result of their lack of shadow. Such is nonsense! They have physicality – why, then, should they be without shadows? And elsewhere it is blamed upon the glow of ectoplasm. I am not even sure I believe in such stuff. And someone described their 'somewhat artificial-looking flatness' – that says everything, does it not?

Yet I wonder if the images I sent to you have undergone some further deterioration that made them unfit to be seen even by the side of these? Those I keep here appear to be a match for them in my eyes, but can I trust them? I admit, it rather gives the lie to that old Yorkshire phrase that is referred to in the book – 'Ah'll believe what ah see.'

But you will forgive me the general tenor of my letter. Please understand that I am simply very distressed at the great opportunity that has been missed. I assure you that I have no desire for personal gain. I never had; I made that quite clear from the outset. I am a Seeker of Truth, and I know that in you and Sir Arthur I found fellow travellers along a similar road, and I cannot contemplate how we have somehow lost each other along the way.

Did Sir Arthur wish to keep the accounts of additional fairy sightings just as the article from last March, ignoring later developments? Had he so little time to commit to creating his new 'epoch' that he was unable to bring the section up to the present? Or did he wish only to protect us and leave us to our misery?

I must go further, for I feel my letter would be half incomplete if I did not mention, not what is missing from the book, but some rather wild matter contained therein. I am no great writer, nor a philosopher. I am not possessed of any special wisdom that lifts me above other men, and yet in the name of common sense, I must address something that I cannot help but feel is disfiguring to the whole. My position as, I hope, your friend and would-be assistant speaks against it, but I must say it; I should feel dishonest if I did not.

I refer to the question of clairvoyance, and its use in detecting the presence of fairies not through the agency of the eye, but the mind. The 'observations' made by a Mr Sergeant (a pseudonymous name, I believe), not only of fairies but undines and wood elves, nymphs, brownies, gnomes and goblins, which fairly seem to have swarmed to Cottingley Glen to meet him in numbers worthy of an invading army, cannot but stretch credulity, particularly as they stand unsupported by any evidence save that of his avowed good character.

I recognise that Sir Arthur has a greater interest in the direction of spiritualism than in fairies, and that the clairvoyant in question is a friend of your own. I mean nothing ill. Rather, in reflecting the accusations that others will make, I hope I merely carry out some small service to the cause in which we are united, or ought to be.

Further – and here I take the risk, I know, of losing your regard entirely, but I must say it – I refer to the explanations provided of the nature and purpose of fairy existence that are put forward by the Theosophists.

Sir, I know that you are a noted member of that organisation, even serving as President of its Blavatsky Lodge, and I am sure they must do much good in the world; I apologise if my comments seem disrespectful. Perhaps it is my own ignorance or lack of understanding, but it seems to me that to describe in such detail the fairy business of making plants grow – with some tending to the leaves, others the roots, and some painting the flowers their various colours – is more than a little fanciful. We have scarcely proved the reality of fairies before unveiling them as the vital link between the sun's energy and leaf!

Furthermore, the book explains the different species of fairy required for the numerous tasks involved in making a plant grow, and puts down their method to that mysterious concept of 'magnetism'. How could we know such things? We are describing the dark side of the moon by the means of a match! Such categorisation can surely withstand no serious questioning.

I do not wish to trample upon your beliefs – indeed, I am sure in other aspects it must be a very admirable system – but this is very wild, and surely has no place within a serious approach to the subject. And for you to say, after hearing about all my experiences, that the fairies do not die as we do…!

But I will leave it there, at the risk of alienating you for ever. I hope you will forgive my consternation and give credence to my genuine intentions. I simply feel that something of a steadier and more closely observed nature would have had greater efficacy. But perhaps Sir Arthur felt, as he says somewhere, 'The human race does not deserve fresh evidence, since it has not troubled, as a rule, to examine that which already exists.'

Or – and do I dare hope? –he wishes to stretch the matter to a second volume, filled out with what has befallen us, to strike down the disbelieving critics of the first?

But again, I beg you to have patience with the length of my letter and indeed its manner, for my aim was never to displease you. And I beg you to reply – not only to give any hint of a reason which may be at your disposal as to the omission of my photographs, but to reassure me that I have not trespassed too far upon your tolerance as to be unable to sign myself,

Your humble servant,
Lawrence Fairclough.

12th April 1922

Dear Mr Gardner,

Thank you, wholeheartedly, for your reply. There was no need to apologise for its brevity; the assurance of your continued friendship gave it an import more valuable than any longer missive could impart. I am glad to see that in at least one thing we can fully agree – that in such an enterprise we all must face the severest questioning, and to raise such issues amongst ourselves can be no obstacle compared to that of general disbelief.

But you also make reference to my use of the word 'misery' in my last. It was sharp-eyed of you, and indeed considerate; I thank you for your continuing interest in my little home.

You are right, of course. When I left off, all must have seemed quite content and happy. Charlotte was restored to us, and as blithe and gladsome as may be wished. Harriet had her mother back, just the way she was. I was disappointed in my pictures and bereft of my skeleton but I had my family, and I accepted that – nay, I was grateful for it, and anxious to do nothing else that would risk them. I resolved to never again go to the glen, or to permit them to go either.

Nevertheless, we are in misery – an insidious, creeping, low kind of misery that has stolen upon us, and it is all the more dark because I can see no way out of it.

I have been much thrown together with Harriet in these past few months. She grows a sweet, thoughtful child, always anxious to please her grandpapa, and ever at my side, and though I love to see her there bent over her book or whispering in her dolly's ear, I would that she might prefer to spend a little more time in the company of her mother.

They have not argued. They have not had any quarrel that I know of. Indeed, Harriet is full young to have disagreements of any consequence, or to bear such things running on each day, and yet to observe them is to know that something has come between them. And I must admit that I have felt a growing disinclination for Charlotte's company also, though she smiles if anything more sweetly than she ever did, and professes delight in everything about her.

She sees everything now, of course. There is no impediment to her vision, and yet it strikes me as a shallow sort of seeing, for the warmth of feeling that once accompanied those little glances is absent, and I do not know how to recover it.

She has suffered from her experience of the fairies, of course. I wonder sometimes if she has a variety of shell-shock such as that still faced by many survivors of the war. She no longer likes to sew; she does not read – I could not even persuade her to look over Sir Arthur's book. She picks at her food as if it is distasteful to her, and in consequence she has grown rather thin and wasted. She sits quite still in the evenings and I believe would do so until she were in darkness if I did not suggest that we set a match to the gas-lights. And she gazes steadily out of the window, towards the place where the wind stirs the tops of the trees and describes its unknowable designs in the meadow grass.

If pressed, she tells me that she is happy. And yet – I cannot put it better than this – there is a blankness to her. I do not know what to make of it. Lines from Hartland come back to me: unwelcome lines about changelings and stocks of wood that I wish

I had never read. They have planted images in my mind, and those images mock me and whirl and turn about until everything is confusion. She is *not* a changeling. She is unafraid of the fire; I have watched her most carefully. I have left iron scissors by her chair and she passed them to me when I asked for them. They did not burn her skin; she did not shiver at their touch. Could a changeling attend church? She was there with us even on Christmas, that most holy of days, and she did not flinch. And yet...

Quite recently, I went again to see the woman in the village. Do you remember – the one who did not speak to me, but pushed Hartland's book into my hand? This time I thrust my foot into the door when she attempted to close it in my face. I asked her what she knew of changelings. Do you know what she said to me? 'Dun't dig,' she said. 'Dun't dig where tha dun't want buryin'.'

Burying. It makes me shudder to think of it. Fairies are said to dwell in the hollow hills, are they not? Their home is not in the sun but beneath the rocks, in utterly dark places, away from clean air and the sight of human faces.

When I returned I hurried to find Harriet, but I need not have worried – she had secreted herself behind the door as her mother busied herself about the kitchen. She still cooks, you see, though she eats so little. I myself taste the food carefully to see if she does anything differently now, and I do not detect a change, but how would I remember? It disturbs me to see her at table with us, raising the fork to her lips just as she always did, and yet taking so little, and smiling when she sees me watching.

It means she is staying with us, does it not – that she eats even a little of our food?

Harriet ran to my side at once and stood on tiptoe, as she does when she wants to whisper in my ear. 'She's wishing the butter,' she said, and scurried away as if suddenly afraid.

You see? I believe you have always said that children see the fairies better than anyone. Or has there simply been too much talk of fairies altogether in this house, and we are all cast half into a dream?

But I can tell you nothing definite, there is nothing certain, and so I will turn to Sir Arthur's book, and tell you of some things that have occurred to me since my last reading. Indeed, there are several points that on closer inspection I do not like – things that disturb me greatly, in fact, and I believe it is my duty to bring them to your notice.

There are many mentions of the fairies dancing as an expression of their joy and carelessness, and indeed it is speculated that they only assume a human shape in order to do so, as if such a thing were merely some kind of holiday from their regular existence. I cannot tell you how this troubles me. Something about it makes me shudder, and I do not know what, only that I feel most strongly that it cannot be so.

There is an account given by one gentleman who says he followed a fairy; that it particularly beckoned him onward. Why should a fairy show such interest in the affairs of man? And did it really mean to show him a flint arrowhead when it pointed at the ground? I wonder instead if it intended to lure him to some doorway into the other realm. And there is another case – one 'seen' in the mind by your clairvoyant, it is true, but he says a lovely fairy appeared to one of the girls, wearing an expression 'as if inviting Frances into Fairyland.' Why so? What did it want with her? And what is this land, if it lies beneath the ground?

I am reminded of something Harriet once said: 'They don't really know how to dance. They only wish to make us want to be where they are.'

Then there is the account to which you have referred previously, about the fairies whose beauteous faces became of a sudden as ugly as sin. Hartland speaks of that too, you know – people's grand and beautiful visions of the folk being torn away to reveal 'the most hideous imps of hell'.

When taken against the whole these are hints, mere discordant notes in an otherwise harmonious symphony of pure and lovely beings, but do you not think we should listen to them? Who will hear, if we do not?

And yet that is not all – you know it is not. There is the case simply given as that of Mrs H., who said of a fairy that 'no soul looked through his eyes.' She saw – she saw! Is that what is so wrong, when I look at Charlotte? I do not know, but I wonder.

You see, I think Sir Arthur selects what he will to support his cause and disregards the rest. He believes in the good of all creation. He does not wish to muddy the waters of spiritualism; he wishes the world to believe in a realm of goodness and beauty. He cannot admit the possibility that we have discovered something which is of creation – or perhaps not, as we understand it – but that is dark.

Yet these things creep in. They cannot help being seen in glimpses, like the fairies themselves. One witness even says, 'They are capable individually of becoming extremely attached to humans – or a human – but at any time they may bite you.'

I do not doubt the latter. It is the former I am struggling with. *Are* they capable of such attachment?

Charlotte dresses her daughter. She wipes her face; she directs her in her lessons. But does she *care* for her?

I will watch and I will write to you soon.

Yours,
Lawrence Fairclough.

15th April 1922

Dear Mr Gardner,

You will have been waiting, I am sure, for my letter, though I have not heard from you in the meantime. I shall not wait; I must tell you of my decision.

I have been drawn, night after night, to take up *The Coming of the Fairies* again. That title! In the dark, with nothing outside but the moon riding high and the bats clicking, it could be almost prophetic. Perhaps it is, but then, I have learned to fear other things than those which roam without; it is the ones within that must be watched.

The thing that draws me to the book is this. In your later investigations, you say – or Sir Arthur says – you paid visits to the New Forest and Scotland as well as Yorkshire, speaking to 'fairy lovers and observers' – you do not mention me, of course, but perhaps I no longer fitted your description.

You say that your part in revealing the Cottingley photographs to the world was the worst introduction possible, and that the pictures so used were 'resented as an unwarranted intrusion and desecration'. You present this as a question of local attitude, not mentioning in the slightest my own findings; that the fairies do not like to be watched. But those who know, *know*. Why else would an old lady say to me that I should not dig where I do not wish to be buried?

I cannot bear what they have done to us. I cannot bear the hurt in Harriet's eyes when she turns from her mother; the way she tries and fails to elicit some small sign of love. What can I do, I have vainly asked myself? And yet now I see it was plain before me all along. I must trespass further upon the fairies; I shall publish.

Sir Arthur did not see fit to include my account within his own. What of that? I have no reputation in the literary line, no publishing contact, no idea of where to begin. But what I do have is a story of no less interest than your own, and the determination to see it presented before the world.

And so I have begun. I am currently preparing the text. It is a fact that my photographs no longer hold true; they do not look so much like fairies as creations of the imagination, but that has not prevented others. And I still have the photographs I had the prescience to take of the little skeleton. Some will no doubt say it is nothing more than the partial remains of a tiny bird with a dragonfly's wings appended, but my character, my testimony, shall speak for the truth, as you did for the Wright girl.

I will warn people what they are really like. There shall be no talk of their gladsome frolics and dancing; only of their wickedness.

Charlotte sees what I am about. She thinks I cannot watch her as I once did, but I know! And I see Harriet, her little pensive face as she leans over her book, so pale from keeping indoors. The looks we exchange, when we think her mother does not see – it is all there, all evident.

The world will know. And if you do not believe my proofs are enough – why, I have heard her give herself away, with my own ears! It happened late at night when I thought everyone was abed and I was going over my papers. Her voice came quite plainly from the passage outside my room, low and unlike herself, but perhaps like her true self; the one she hides from us.

'I stung you once,' she said. 'I'll have the rest soon enough.'

And she made chewing sounds with her mouth, as if she was hungry at last – as if she was ravenous, and anticipating the sweet meat of her little daughter.

I rushed out on the instant. She was too quick for me; she was not there.

She is a changeling, I know it now. Oh, I have moments when I doubt; weak moments when I merely think she will end her days in Bedlam with the other lunatics, or perhaps I will. But under such pressures, and quite alone with a child to protect, it is little wonder I experience some confusion. Why, sometimes I wonder if you are indeed who you claim to be, and if Sir Arthur Conan Doyle was ever in receipt of my letter; if you do not keep him apprised, as you promised to do, with all I have to say. I wonder if I have been cruelly deceived in everything – even led astray by a child's fancies, as some would say we *all* have.

But I must hold fast. For something else has struck me: a new idea which would explain all, and indeed show why Sir Arthur has not deigned to call upon me – why he would not dare show his face!

He has set out to offer serious proofs of fairy existence. He has presented himself as describing all that science can bring to matters of a spiritual nature. And yet he has so subtly interwoven his facts with stuff clearly discoverable as fiction as to deliberately undermine his own arguments.

The fairies, he says, appear stiff and frozen in the Cottingley photographs because they move so very slowly. I know this to be a blatant untruth. One of their 'apparently pencilled' faces is simply made to appear so by the outline of her hair. His eye-witnesses see them only in the derangement of the full sun or when they have been fasting.

He notes in passing the coincidence that the Wright girl's family was already 'inclined to occult study'. He happens to mention that the elder child is imaginative, even dreamy, that she often spent her leisure hours drawing fairies, and that she was apprenticed for a time to a firm of photographers. He states that even her father asked the girls how they faked the pictures.

One would almost think that he did not *wish* to be believed.

Of course, Sir Arthur does not overtly draw attention to these matters. He is too experienced for that. He simply presents them all, and indeed his own doubts, as things that could easily be overcome, and allows people to read into it what they will.

Here is the rub. Did he think no one would see through it? Did he think himself like his character, his Sherlock Holmes, building an unassailable wall of rationality? But I do see through it. I think Sir Arthur has purposely chosen examples of sightings that are poorer than mine. He has inserted passages of absurd surmise quite knowingly.

It all culminates in the half-crazed comments from Bishop Leadbeater. He talks of the orange and purple fairies of Sicily, black and white ones of the Dakotas, the sky blue ones of Australia, and, more risibly, the gleaming crimson fairies resembling the metal orichalcum – the *what*, Sir? – of the Atlanteans.

Can anyone read this and not suspect? I see it now more clearly than ever. Why, when Sir Arthur writes that a high development of intellect is a bar to psychic perception, he must have been laughing down his sleeve!

It is pure nonsense, Sir, and I tell you, I know the reason why. It is not some mischief that is at the root of it all, but fear.

Sir Arthur had taken on a sacred trust and was unequal to the task. And I think the key lies not with Elsie Wright and Frances Griffiths, but with another girl: and she, entirely blind.

The one I mean is, of course, Miss Eva Longbottom, of whom Sir Arthur writes at length in *The Coming of the Fairies*. Her claims of seeing the little folk clairvoyantly, whilst being completely blind, make her particularly easy to dismiss; and yet I sense the truth in her words. That fairy music is something of itself and untranslatable has the unmistakeable ring of authenticity. For a person without sight to gain the impression of dancing 'without any tangles in it' has also, and if I do not deceive myself, her account of fairies singing in their colours has enough of the peculiar to convince.

No: it is not her visions that I doubt, but the claim that the young lady was blind from birth.

That, I do not believe. How else would she know what colours are? I think that she was struck blind, sir, for spying upon the fairies; and it is that, more than any other threat, implied or obvious, that has made Sir Arthur draw back from a more convincing disclosure. He has learned enough to discover that his fascination could come at a high cost and he has turned aside. He has glimpsed their true nature. Even as I write I seem to recall something that was said in *The Strand* about their 'grotesque, unmeaning tricks', though I do not think he embellished such a statement with any detail – that is telling in itself, is it not?

He had committed to publish, but he did not want to be believed: not because the fairies were *not* real, but because he knew they *were* – yet different to how he imagined them to be.

I cannot entirely blame him. What *are* these things we seek so heedlessly? I do not know, and would not claim to. But they are loathsome creatures, and we have reason to fear them. Yes, I see through it; he *has* brought certain truths before the eye of the world, even if they are not the ones he intended.

I, sir, shall not flinch from my undertaking to do the rest. I return to my books.

Yours sincerely,
Lawrence Fairclough.

19th April 1922

Dear Mr Gardner,

Sir, I must protest. You know me too well by now, at least from my letters, to make such accusations, no matter how tactfully couched. Does Sir Arthur Conan Doyle know himself to be sane, despite the accusations he has brought down upon his head by publishing his book? Well, I know myself to be sane, and after all your investigations, you should know better than to call it into question.

I recognise that you have been overwhelmed by a tide of fanciful reports following the article in *The Strand*. That is surely no response, nor an excuse for omitting an account of such importance. I realise that it was entirely the great man's choice, but I question whether he has been entirely level in making it.

No matter. I realise I have unwittingly insulted you by questioning your integrity, and indeed that you are whom you claim to be. It was not my intention. I have simply been honest enough to relay every doubt that has assailed me; clearly, this was one I had long overcome. I see that conveying it to you has not illuminated the situation, and I would have better left it unsaid.

As for Miss Eva Longbottom really being blind from a baby,

and the claim that she receives great joy from the fairy presences all about – well, perhaps that is what you have been told. Men (and women) said to be of equal character to mine are not immune to the occasional untruth; and it is possible they may be mistaken. I merely paraphrase your own words.

That is all I shall say, save this: no matter what there is to fear or dread, no matter what ridicule I face from those who should know better, I will not be turned aside from this important work.

I shall trouble you no more.

Sincerely,
Mr L. H. Fairclough.

21st April 1922

My dear Mr Gardner,

Pray, forgive the tone of my last. I regret it most earnestly. I dare say you did not expect to hear from me again, and you would not do so were it not a matter of the utmost urgency, indeed, possibly of life or death – or worse than either, as it may well turn out to be.

I have little time to waste, and yet I must leave a record in the event that some terrible thing may befall us. Indeed, I think it has already befallen us, and it is too late – but soon I shall don my coat and go once more to the glen, and see what I may, and end this where I must.

She is gone from me – little Harriet is gone. I shall endeavour to restrain my feelings, and my rapidly scrawling pen, and explain myself as a rational man.

It began this morning. Charlotte was in the kitchen, as she so often is, and Harriet was peeping from behind the door. Charlotte was butchering a rabbit. She was making a stew, and humming some strange air, so quietly it was beyond recognition. She kept stopping – the strokes of her knife against the board would cease and the tune would pass beyond hearing, and after a few moments would begin again. Perhaps she was listening to the child breathing; who knows?

Of a sudden, I heard her stepping towards the door. And then she said, in a too-sweet voice, 'Do you watch me, child?'

I set down my pen at once. I hurried into the passage to see Harriet staring up at her mother, her eyes wide, and not saying a word. Charlotte in turn stared at the child, her eyes a fixed gleam in her awful thin face. She never once shifted her gaze to me. She clutched the knife in her hand and blood dripped from it to the floor, but I was the only one who noticed.

Then Charlotte leaned over her daughter, and she raised the knife and said, 'I shall put both your eyes out of your head.'

I cannot describe the effect of her words. It was not just their intent but the way they were spoken, so cold, so *true*– but Harriet could not move. It was I who had to catch her arm and pull her away, to turn her from the sight of her mother's ugly staring, because she was entranced; I would almost say she was under some spell.

It broke when I pulled her back and knelt before her. She cried, then; indeed, you may only imagine her distress. I tried to soothe her, though I did not really know how, and with my shaking hands and unsteady voice – but I did what I could, which is all that any of us can do.

I know what you will say. You will think Charlotte's words were suggested by her own recent experiences or by her fancies, and that the memory of it will quickly fade. You would say she will soon be well again. But I heard the way she spoke, and saw the way she looked, and I cannot doubt the truth.

All the time I comforted her child, I felt Charlotte watching us. And in her demeanour she betrayed – oh, from her stance I would have thought it amusement, but it was not even that; there was only the most terrible indifference.

If I had doubted before, I could not do so then. But she still held the knife, and I must confess I was afraid.

I did not heat the poker and describe the sign of the cross upon her forehead. I did not slip a Prayer Book under her pillow or douse her with holy water or hold her before the fire to trick her into betraying herself. I did none of those things – curse my useless hands! I told Harriet to run along and read her book and not bother her mama, and I straightened to see that Charlotte had already gone. The sound of a knife on wood came once more from the kitchen, and I wondered what kind of stew she would *like* to make; I wondered if she would eat it all up.

I sat before my work, and looked upon it, and despaired. I do not know how much time passed, but it was not until later that I thought to look in on Harriet. She was gone, of course.

She had left only a note behind:

They took my mama. I am going to find her.

And beneath:

I think I hurt the fairy lady with my stick.

At once I saw her in my mind's eye, poking beneath each rock and branch in the glen, only to meet with – what? Had the little maid been waiting there – had she been in health when Harriet came along and unwittingly discovered her? But the child was innocent. She had intended no harm. Had she truly caused the little fairy's death with her poking and prying? It could not be!

But then all their mischief, all their revenge, would really be intended for the child. And she had gone once more to the glen – gone into their hands! What if, this time, she did not come back?

What if she *did* come back?

I cannot express to you my horror at the thought. Harriet, lost to me for ever – or Harriet returning, her feet browned with earth, scratching on the door perhaps at midnight, the eyes that were so like her father's as black as sloes. Harriet without the enlivening principle that makes her truly herself – without an ounce of love in her!

What might the wicked little creatures do to my true grandchild, if she fell into their hands – if she had really done them such an injury as she suspected? You will see it all, I suppose. For perhaps this was the reason our encounter with the fairies was not like that of other people, or some of them. I do not know if they think like we do, if they have any system of morality we could recognise. I had not imagined that they discriminate: I had thought their punishment had fallen to all of us, my son's wife more than anyone, but perhaps it is not yet finished.

It was Harriet who injured the fairy. It was I who carried the little body away. I cannot keep away from them, of course. I am going to seek them in the glen – the real Charlotte, with her eyes as soft and warm as they used to be, and my own sweet Harriet, unchanged, throwing her arms about my neck. I fear it may already be too late. For time is said to pass differently in the fairy realm, and if they have eaten of their food – what then?

Fairies are said to steal humans away and leave changelings in their place in order to strengthen their line. Will I find Charlotte big with a fairy child? Or Harriet being raised a fairy? How would a human ever become one of those frail little beings – or is there some race of fairy I have not yet seen? I cannot imagine it at all. For the thing that divides us is surely the possession of a soul, and how could that difference be surmounted, unless they have by some means removed it from them?

I fear I am to go somewhere not of earth or of heaven or of hell, but somewhere that is different from them all. It is a terrible choice, and I pray you never have to make one like it. For I do not now think I will ever see my son or my wife again, even in the next world, as has been the dearest hope of my life. A course lies ahead that is entirely new and strange and different to me. But I know my son would tell me, unhesitatingly, to go – to protect his daughter. And I will, for she is alone, and a child, and lost, and I can do no other thing.

I will try to follow where she has gone. I will take a Bible, and, I believe, the iron scissors. And if I find the false child first – then, I can only trust that I shall know what to do.

Here before me is the price of my fascination. Sir Arthur has felt a little of it too, I think. His was the world's censure; mine – ah, but who knows what that shall be? I do not know if I will be blinded or stolen away, or worse – for what could they want with an old man? And what could be more terrible than what they have already done?

How strange it is that I find you are the only one I can tell. I have almost finished my letter – all that stands between me and them – and when I set out I shall leave it on the table. Perchance someone will find it and post it to you. Perhaps that someone might even be me. Perhaps their hands, their face, will only look like mine. Who can say?

Nothing remains but to sign myself, now and I hope ever your friend,

Lawrence.

About the Author

Alison Littlewood's latest novel is *The Hidden People*, published by Jo Fletcher Books. Set in Victorian rural society, it is about the murder of a young girl suspected of being a fairy changeling. Her first book, *A Cold Season*, was selected for the Richard and Judy Book Club and described as 'perfect reading for a dark winter's night.' Her sequel, *A Cold Silence*, has recently been published, along with a *Zombie Apocalypse!* novel, *Acapulcalypse Now*. Her other books are *Path of Needles*, a dark blend of fairy tales and crime fiction, and *The Unquiet House*, a ghost story set in the Yorkshire countryside.

Alison's short stories have been picked for *Best British Horror*, *The Best Horror of the Year*, *The Year's Best Dark Fantasy and Horror* and *The Mammoth Book of Best New Horror* anthologies, as well as *The Best British Fantasy* and *The Mammoth Book of Best British Crime*. They have been gathered together in her collections *Quieter Paths* and in *Five Feathered Tales*, a collaboration with award-winning illustrator Daniele Serra. She won the 2014 Shirley Jackson Award for Short Fiction.

Alison lives with her partner Fergus in Yorkshire, England, in a house of creaking doors and crooked walls. She loves exploring the hills and dales with her two hugely enthusiastic Dalmatians and has a penchant for books on folklore and weird history, Earl Grey tea and semicolons. You can talk to her on Twitter: @Ali__L, see her on Facebook or visit her at: www.alisonlittlewood.co.uk.

Author's Acknowledgements

One hundred years ago, when Elsie and Frances first captured fairies on a photographic plate, they essentially pictured a very Victorian kind of fairy. (Many years later, they admitted using cardboard cut-outs propped up with hatpins.) Their pretty winged creations had largely replaced the older tales of darker, more dangerous creatures, who might even steal humans away. It has been enormous fun bringing the different strands of lore together, and I am grateful for the work of the folklorists and researchers who have made it possible. I am also indebted to *The Science of Fairy Tales: An Inquiry into Fairy Mythology* by Edwin Sidney Hartland (1891) and *The Coming of the Fairies* by Sir Arthur Conan Doyle (March 1922).

Many are surprised that Doyle, creator of the ever-rational Sherlock Holmes, also argued for the existence of fairies (and indeed in favour of spiritualism). In a way, though, he was simply attempting to apply scientific methods to unscientific matters. However outlandish his occupations, his aim was noble: he wished to increase our knowledge, to provide comfort against the fear of death and ultimately, to better the lot of humankind. In the words of Harry Price, he was 'a giant in stature with the heart of a child' – and who isn't the better for that? This volume is dedicated to his memory, with admiration and respect.

I would also like to thank Ian Whates for prompting me to write a novella, something I rarely do. He is definitely one of the good guys, and is no doubt at the root of many creative endeavours that would not otherwise exist. I'd also like to thank my fellow contributor to this novella series, Simon Clark. It was through a similar request from him, for a Sherlock Holmes short story, that I first became interested in Sir Arthur and his work.

Newcon Press Novellas, Set 2

Simon Clark / Alison Littlewood / Sarah Lotz / Jay Caselberg

Cover art by Vincent Sammy

Case of the Bedevilled Poet ~ His life under threat, poet Jack Crofton flees through the streets of war-torn London. He seeks sanctuary in a pub and falls into company with two elderly gentlemen who claim to be the real Holmes and Watson. Unconvinced but desperate, Jack shares his story, and Holmes agrees to take his case…

Cottingley ~ A century after the world was rocked by news that two young girls had photographed fairies in the sleepy village of Cottingley, we finally learn the true nature of these fey creatures. Correspondence has come to light; a harrowing account written by village resident Lawrence Fairclough that lays bare the fairies' sinister malevolence.

Body in the Woods ~ When an old friend turns up on Claire's doorstep one foul night and begs for her help, she knows she should refuse, but she owes him and, despite her better judgement, finds herself helping to bury something in the woods. Will it stay buried, and can Claire live with the knowledge of what she did that night?

The Wind ~ Having moved to Abbotsford six months ago, Gerry reckons he's getting used to country life and the rural veterinary practice he's taken on. Nothing prepared him, though, for the strange wind that springs up to stir the leaves in unnatural fashion, nor for the strikingly beautiful woman the villagers are so reluctant to talk about…

THE ION RAIDER
Ian Whates
The Dark Angels (Volume 2)
Cover art by Jim Burns

The much anticipated follow-up to the Amazon best seller *Pelquin's Comet*.

"A good, unashamed, rip-roaring piece of space opera that hits the spot."
— *Financial Times*

"He's a natural story-teller and works his material with verve, obvious enjoyment, and an effortlessly breezy prose style."
— *The Guardian*

"*Pelquin's Comet* is classic space opera at its finest, a satisfying and enjoyable novel in its own right and an intriguing introduction to a story universe I want to visit again. Thoroughly recommended."
— *SFCrowsnest*

"Whates does a good job playing out the lines of suspense while steadily revealing significant plot points, keeping things character-focused… It's a fast, fun read." — *Speculation*

"You won't go far wrong with this book... you never know, it could be the beginning of something wonderful." — *Booklore*

~

Leesa is determined to find out who is quietly assassinating her old crewmates, the Dark Angels, and stop them before it's her turn to die.

First Solar Bank have sent **Drake** on his most dangerous mission yet, to the isolationist world of Enduril, where nothing is as it seems.

Jen just wanted to be left in peace on her farm, until somebody blew the farm up. She escaped, a fact those responsible will come to regret.

Released May 2017 www.newconpress.co.uk

IMMANION PRESS

Purveyors of Speculative Fiction

www.immanion-press.com

The Lightbearer by Alan Richardson

Michael Horsett parachutes into Occupied France before the D-Day Invasion. He is dropped in the wrong place, miles from the action, badly injured, and totally alone. He falls prey to two Thelemist women who have awaited the Hawk God's coming, attracts a group of First World War veterans who rally to what they imagine is his cause, is hunted by a troop of German Field Police who are desperate to find him, and has a climactic encounter with a mutilated priest who believes that Lucifer Incarnate has arrived...

The Lightbearer is a unique Gnostic thriller, dealing with the themes of Light and Darkness, Good and Evil, Matter and Spirit.

"The Lightbearer is another shining example of Alan Richardson's talent as a story-teller. An unusual and gripping war story with more facets than a star sapphire." – Mélusine Draco, author of "Aubry's Dog" and "Black Horse, White Horse". ISBN: 978-1-907737-63-3 £11.99 $18.99

Dark in the Day, Ed. by Storm Constantine & Paul Houghton

Weirdness lurks beyond the margins of the mundane, emerging to dismantle our assumptions of reality. Dark in the Day is an anthology of weird fiction, penned by established writers and also those new to the genre – the latter being authors who are, or were, students of Creative Writing at Staffordshire University, where editor Storm Constantine occasionally delivers guest lectures. Her co-editor, Paul Houghton, is the senior lecturer in Creative Writing at the university.

Contributors include: Martina Bellovičová, J. E. Bryant, Glynis Charlton, Storm Constantine, Louise Coquio, Elizabeth Counihan, Krishan Coupland, Elizabeth Davidson, Siân Davies, Paul Finch, Rosie Garland, Rhys Hughes, Kerry Fender, Andrew Hook, Paul Houghton, Tanith Lee, Tim Pratt, Nicholas Royle, Michael Marshall Smith, Paula Wakefield, Ian Whates and Liz Williams.

ISBN: 978-1-907737-74-9 £11.99, $18.99

Lightning Source UK Ltd.
Milton Keynes UK
UKOW05f2044300617

304458UK00001B/132/P